Covering Christmas

George Friederick

Bessie Pease Gutmann

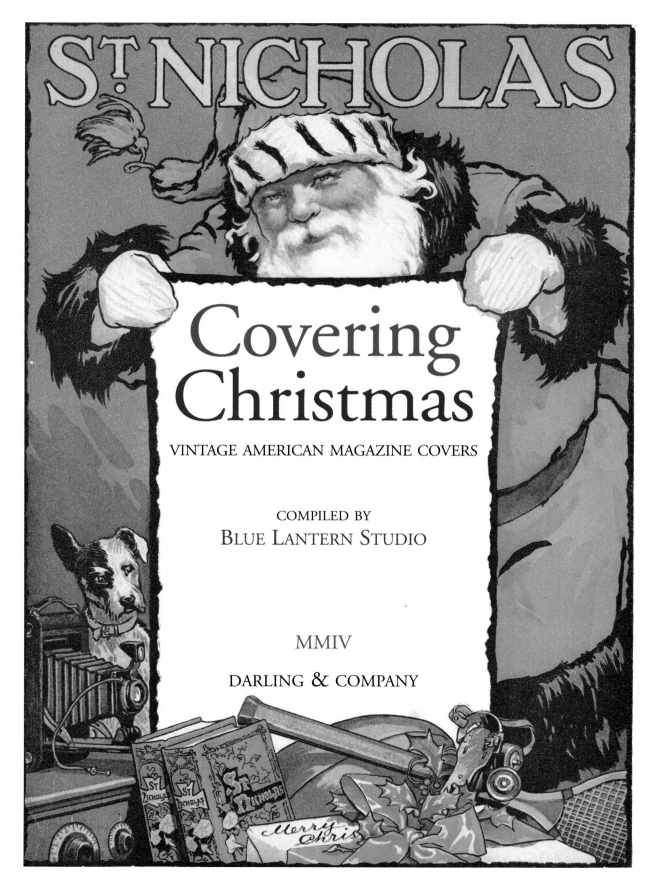

St. Nicholas

Covering
Christmas

VINTAGE AMERICAN MAGAZINE COVERS

COMPILED BY
BLUE LANTERN STUDIO

MMIV

DARLING & COMPANY

Copyright © 2004 Blue Lantern Studio
All rights reserved First printing Printed in Singapore

ISBN 1-59583-003-0

DARLING & COMPANY

A division of Laughing Elephant

3645 Interlake Avenue North Seattle Washington 98103

www.LAUGHINGELEPHANT.com

Forward

The American magazine, which flourished most richly in the first half of the twentieth century, was a powerful force for enlightenment and, at the same time, homogeneity. Most homes bought or had subscriptions for several magazines, many of which were weeklies. The average home had a magazine rack which was constantly being filled and emptied. The differences between newspapers, which also abounded at this time, and magazines was that newspapers were first of all concerned with daily happenings and magazines with perspective. Newspapers were primarily a matter of words, and magazines had many pictures. At the beginning of the twentieth century, magazines were primarily illustrated with paintings and drawings, even though photography was readily available, easier and cheaper to use. As the century advanced, photography continually gained in favor, and by mid-century was largely dominant. The reasons for the early preference for art over photographs and the gradual shift of favor are subtle.

The cover of each magazine was of great importance then, as it is today. Magazine sales could vary by hundreds of thousands of copies according to the popularity of the cover image. In light of this, it is hardly surprising that editors strove to get the finest artists possible, pay them handsomely, and direct them to subjects of the widest popular appeal.

Christmas was, as now, an important holiday, and magazine sales were highest in December. December covers were thus the year's greatest challenge, and Christmas was their overwhelming subject.

We offer here some of our favorite holiday covers. No photographic covers are included. These covers represent American illustration at a high point, and also offer a synthesis of American Christmas traditions.

We have assembled the covers by theme, and within each theme they are presented chronologically.

This is a highly selective group of images. Thousands of covers were produced in this period; many were uninspired. The magazines with the largest circulations commanded the best talent. We have tried to offer as much variety as possible, but our quest for excellence led us again and again to select covers from a relatively small group of publications.

Welleran Poltarnees

# Looking Forward to Christmas

For children, anticipation is the sweetest part of the Christmas season. For weeks, or even months, a child's inner life is likely to be irradiated with the Christmas to come. Dreams are, of course, haunted with visions of Santa Claus and the ideal gifts which he will bring. Every day a child is liable to be struck, as by lightning, with a prevision of the glorious future. For adults the feelings are more muted, and desire is underlain by the weight of responsibility. The holiday season is the focus of the commercial year, the familial year, and the celebratory year. It is the harbor at journey's end; a dream of perfection in our daily lives in which we will get everything right and where our inner selves will be revealed in their purity. Christmas is a utopia which we yearn towards with ever fresh enthusiasm, despite the impossibility of its living up to our dreams of what it might be.

MUNSEY

CHRISTMAS

THE FRANK A. MUNSEY COMPANY
NEW YORK AND LONDON

PRICE
15
CENTS

Unknown

Robert John Wildhack

THE PEOPLE'S HOME JOURNAL

CHRISTMAS · 1915 · FIVE CENTS

F. M. LUPTON, Publisher, NEW YORK

Katherine R. Wireman

Neysa McMein

COUNTRY GENTLEMAN

1934 DECEMBER 10¢
15¢ IN CANADA
INCLUDING TAX

Hy Hintermeister

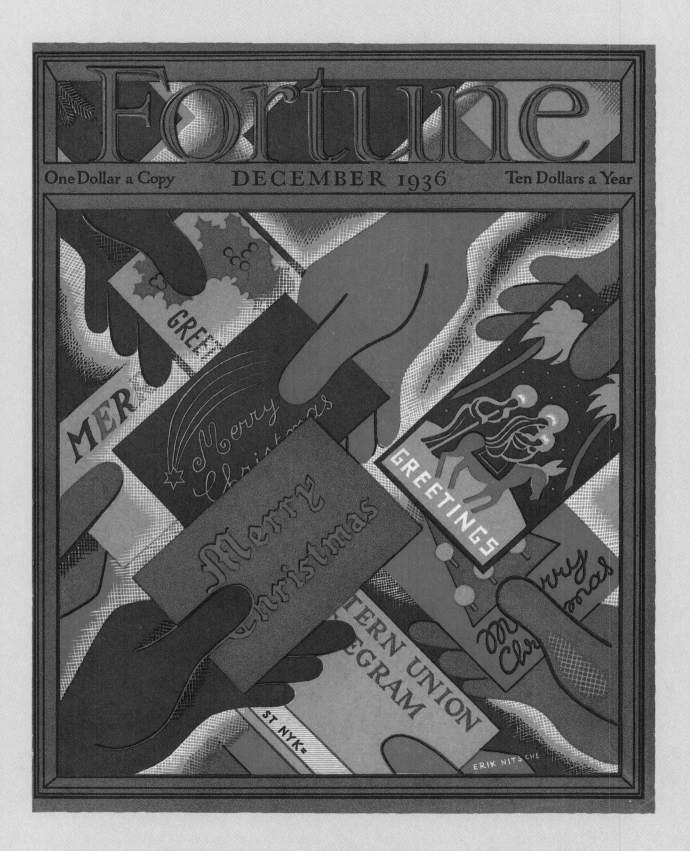

Erik Nitsche

F. Hook

Christmas Shopping

Shopping has a bad reputation. The common belief is that it is a primitive manifestation of crass self-indulgence, the triumph of materialistic values. This is, of course, partly true, but this mundane activity is partially redeemed by the fact that our spirits work through the physical world, groping towards structure and beauty through a reordering of things of the world.

Christmas shopping is the noblest of all shopping experiences, for it is dedicated to the wants and needs of others. We plan and worry so that those we love might be made happier. We ask ourselves day and night what this person might want that they do not already have. We search for items that will delight their deepest beings, items which they have denied themselves, or have not yet discovered. We worry and plan. We neglect our other responsibilities, so that we may search for perfect gifts. We brave crowds of others similarly intent on this quest. We spend more than we can afford, then, as Christmas approaches we start to panic for the perfect gifts we seek elude us. We do all of this because convention forces it upon us, and because we wish to manifest our love.

The Christmas
Ladies' Home Journal

December, 1911
Fifteen Cents

The Curtis
Publishing Company
Philadelphia

CORWIN KNAPP LINSON

Corwin Knapp Linson

Helen Dryden

S. Gulbransen

Hildegard M. Woodward

Hazel Frazee

LADIES' HOME
JOURNAL

DECEMBER, 1928

Volume XLV, Number 12

THE CURTIS PUBLISHING COMPANY, PHILADELPHIA

10 Cents By subscription $1.00. In the United States and in Canada

C.E. Chambers

Country Life

Sophie Wilson

Dec. 1929

Price 50¢

The Christmas Annual

Doubleday Doran & Co. Inc.

Sophie Wilson

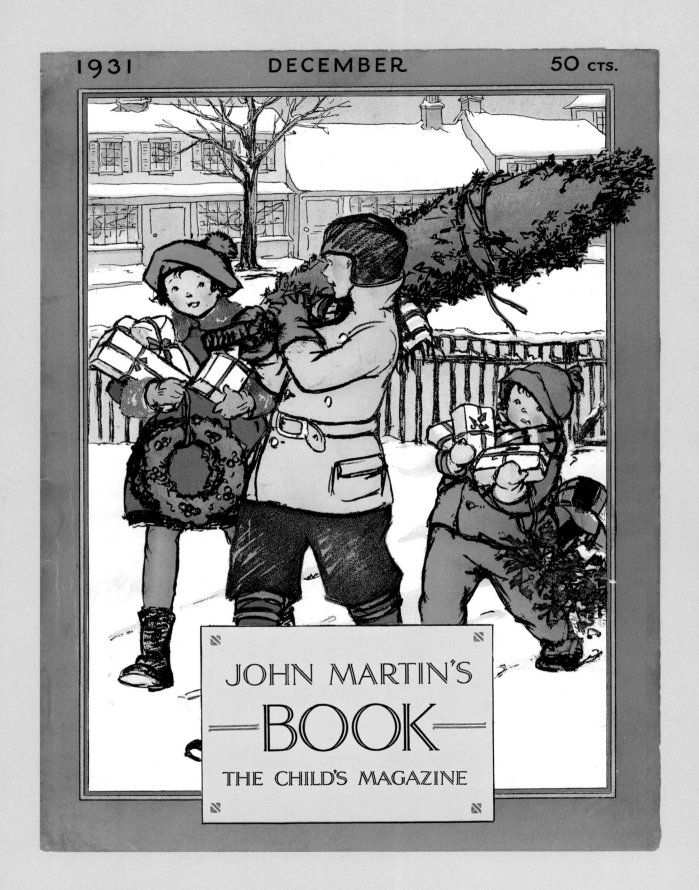

JOHN MARTIN'S
-=BOOK=-
THE CHILD'S MAGAZINE

DECEMBER 1932 ★ 10 CENTS

BETTER HOMES
& GARDENS

Meredith Publishing Company-Des Moines, Iowa
More Than 1,400,000 Circulation

21

Edwin P. Couse

Maginel Wright Barney

22

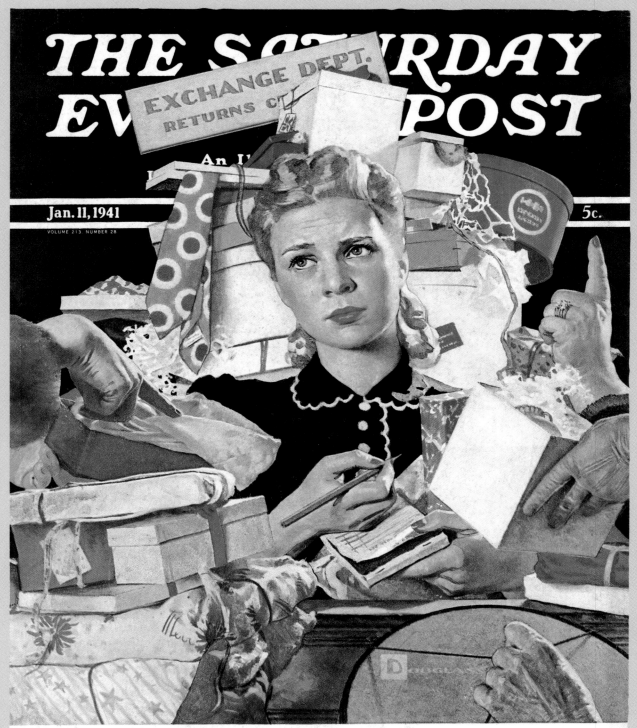

THE SATURDAY EVENING POST

EXCHANGE DEPT.
RETURNS C

An Il

Jan. 11, 1941

VOLUME 213. NUMBER 28

5c.

INSIDE GERMAN EUROPE By DEMAREE BESS

Douglas Crockwell

Decorating the Home

It is strange how little most of us decorate our homes throughout the year. A wedding, a graduation, or an elaborate party may stir us to decorate, but these are rare occasions. Christmas and Halloween are the only times custom forces most of us to make an effort to make our joy visible. We don't see the inside of most peoples' homes, but we do see the outsides of them, and other than these two holidays how much seasonal adornment do we see? Christmas lights, which make many places lovely that were not so otherwise, are taken down in early January, and not replaced with lights of other colors, for other moods or situations. When Christmas has passed we face months of ordinary homes, bare windows and empty porches. It would be lovely if we put seasonal wreaths on our front doors, but how few of us do. We do enjoy the transfigured neighborhoods of Christmas.

M?CALL'S MAGAZINE

CHRISTMAS

NUMBER

DECEMBER, 1911

FIVE CENTS A COPY
FIFTY CENTS A YEAR

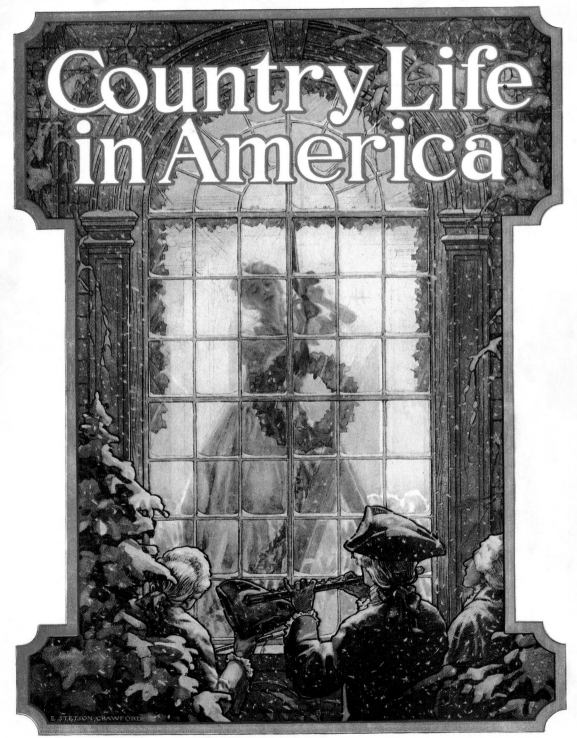

The Christmas
WOMAN'S HOME
COMPANION

Eugenie Wireman

Torre Bevans

DECEMBER 22, 1921 PRICE 15 CENTS

The Conspirators

Herbert Paus

The YOUTH'S COMPANION
combined with

American Boy

Founded 1827

DECEMBER 1935

10¢

One Year $1.00

COVER PAINTING BY EDGAR FRANKLIN WITTMACK

Three Years $2.00

A Jules Verne Story of the Outer Spaces
"PLUM DUFF" *by* PETER van DRESSER

Edgar Franklin Wittmack

34

John Falter

The Christmas Tree

The Christmas tree is a powerful symbol, and a marvelous part of our holiday celebration. It is startling to realize that it has only been with us since the 18th century, and only prevalent since the mid-19th century. It is right that an evergreen be chosen, for it is fully itself in midwinter, but how strange that we should cut it down and bring it into our homes. Once there, it does counteract winter's chill with its lovely odor, persistent vitality and wonderful structure. How odd it is that we have come to decorate it with glistening spheres and little figures of glass. The final wonderful touch is the lights, which glow and reflect, creating a surreal object in the middle of our staid rooms. How grateful we should be for this elaborate tradition, and yet, as many of the best things of life, we are blinded by familiarity to the glories around us.

House & Garden

CHRISTMAS HOUSE NUMBER

DECEMBER 1917   CONDÉ NAST *Publisher*   25 CENTS

Ethel F.B. Bains

THE DELINEATOR

DECEMBER 1925

FROM PAINTING BY J. SCOTT WILLIAMS

In this issue "AND ON EARTH—PEACE" *by Zona Gale*

KATHLEEN NORRIS   ELLIS PARKER BUTLER   DIXIE WILLSON

FASHIONS FOR MIDWINTER AND THE HOLIDAYS

TWENTY CENTS
THE COPY

THE BUTTERICK PUBLISHING COMPANY, NEW YORK, N. Y., U. S. A.

$2.00 A YEAR
$2.50 IN CANADA

HOUSE & GARDEN

December - 1926

Christmas Gifts in this Issue

35 cts. - 3.50 a year

39

Richardson

DECEMBER 1931

10 CENTS

DELINEATOR

KATHLEEN NORRIS   CONINGSBY DAWSON   LADY ELEANOR SMITH

SUNSET

December · 1932   10 Cents

This issue goes to more than 200,000 of the Best Homes in the West.

HOUSE BEAUTIFUL

COMBINED WITH HOME & FIELD

DECEMBER 1934 · PRICE 35 CENTS
40 cents in Canada

NRA
CODE

Leon Carroll

Arthur Crouch

The Saturday Evening

POST

December 22, 1951 — 15¢

THE TRUTH ABOUT THE
BLACK MARKET IN BABIES

Uncle Sam's Bouncers
Get Tough

By RICHARD ENGLISH

Stevan Dohanos

The Saturday Evening

POST

December 27, 1952 — 15¢

**OUR BABY WAS
BORN BLIND**
By Frank M. Stevenson

**I Fly the Night Skies
Over Korea**
By a Navy Pilot

Stevan Dohanos

# Santa Claus

Santa is currently out of favor. Too many parents, blinded by shallow rationality, discourage in their children a belief in Santa Claus. I think Salvation Army Santas and department store Santas were a large mistake. Their ordinariness, their too frequently pitiful masquerade, have not helped the image of this noble figure. He should have been left as a mystery– sounds heard on the roof, glimpses of color in the night sky, milk consumed and cookie crumbs left behind. We should have left it to the poets and visionaries to tell us about him. He is the embodiment of generosity, laboring all year– with the help of his elves– to make toys for all the children of the world. His omniscience, his power to visit every home in one night, his sled drawn through the sky by eight reindeer– all of these constitute a magical being both profound and good. He makes Christmas sweeter.

December 20 1913

Five Cents the Copy

The COUNTRY GENTLEMAN

The OLDEST AGRICULTURAL JOURNAL in the WORLD

The CURTIS PUBLISHING COMPANY Philadelphia

Chas. A. MacLellan

A BEAUTIFUL PATRIOTIC CHRISTMAS NUMBER

PICTORIAL REVIEW

Full of
Xmas Features
for Young and Old
Xmas Cards
Double Page Cut Out
2 Xmas Pictures
by Arthur I. Keller
etc. etc.
18 Pages in Color

DECEMBER 1918

TWENTY CENTS

Guy Hoff

48

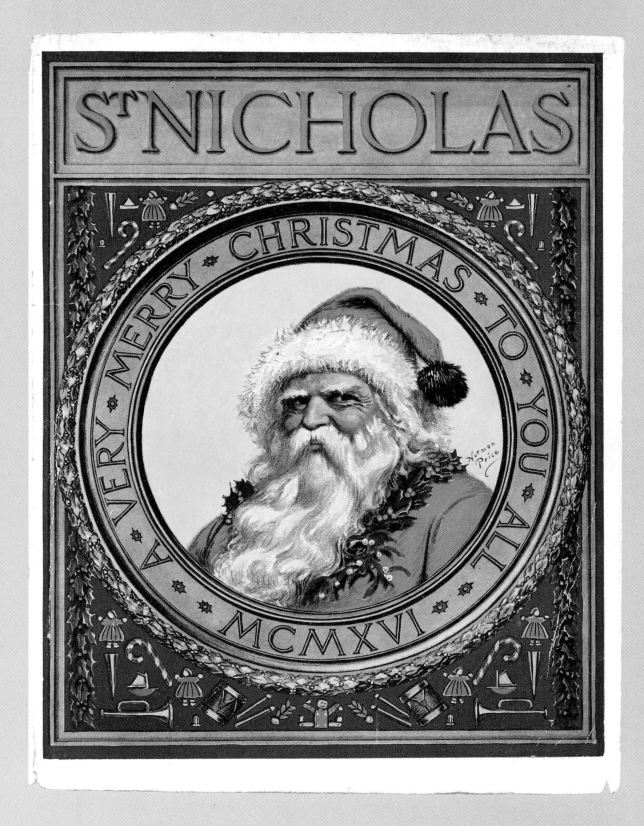

49

THE SATURDAY EVENING POST

An Illustrated Weekly
Founded 1728 by Benj. Franklin

Vol. 193, No. 26. Published Weekly at Philadelphia. Entered as Second-Class Matter, November 18, 1879, at the Post Office at Philadelphia, Under the Act of March 3, 1879.

DEC. 25, 1920

5c. THE COPY
10c. in Canada

Hugh MacNair Kahler — Kennett Harris — Nina Wilcox Putnam
Will Irwin — Hugh Wiley — Corinne Lowe — F. Britten Austin

J.C. Leyendecker

The Johnsons

Frances Tipton Hunter

Phillip Little

DECEMBER 1931   35 CENTS

CHILD LIFE

The Children's Own Magazine

OATS

KEITH WARD

MERRY CHRISTMAS!

RAND McNALLY & COMPANY, *Publishers*

Keith Ward

Paolo Garretto

HOLIDAY

DECEMBER 1956 · 50c

THE MIDDLE EAST   SOUTH CAROLINA   NAPLES, FLORIDA   EXETER

57

Andre Tiancon

Gift Giving

The dream that sustained us through the challenge of shopping is now tested by the giving of the gift. It is a fine thing that we wrap our gifts. It not only creates the tension of delay, but also additional loveliness in our homes. Each gift is wrapped in colored or decorated paper, and then tied up with colored ribbon or cord. A group of such packages, varied in shape, size and color and piled together, create a visual phantasmagoria such as seldom occurs in our lives. As the gifts are distributed we doubt for a moment that we have chosen correctly. A toaster-oven or terrycloth bathrobe no longer seems as right and unusual as we had imagined them. We anxiously await the reaction of the recipient. The unwrapping can be agonizingly tense, especially with the young or old who fumble with the ribbon. Then what we have given is revealed to everyone, especially to the person for whom we designed this moment, and our goal is achieved.

THE UNJUST JUDGE By JOHN LUTHER LONG IN THIS NUMBER

SUCCESS
MAGAZINE

CHRIST-
-MAS
1909

PUBLISHED BY THE SUCCESS COMPANY, NEW YORK 10c. a Copy $1.00 a Year

F.L. Stoddard

Frank X. Leyendecker

Woman's Home Companion

December 1927   Ten Cents

CHRISTMAS NUMBER

61   Maginel Wright Barney

Gift Receiving

It is even harder to play the role of gift receiver than that of gift bestower. As one hesitates over the wrappings, trying not to barbarize what may have been labored over, we realize that the delay is causing the giver increased anxiety. Once opened we are expected to respond. "Just what I wanted" seems insincere. Too exuberant a reaction also rings falsely. "How interesting" suggests the gift is puzzling, probably unwanted. Unwanted gifts are the most difficult challenge. Do we vigorously lie, or do we try to shift the focus away from ourselves to the item itself? Children are almost always openhearted in their reactions, which can hurt, but at least the giver knows how they did.

After the gifts are all opened there is an immediate letdown – for both the giver and receiver– for there is always a discrepancy between our hopes or intentions and reality. As we grow wise in giving and receiving we realize that what we had imagined was a hackneyed phrase is actually a deep truth– it is the thought that counts.

Magazine covers understandably picture happy gift receiving. Only the Leyendecker on page 74 gives us any sense of the poignancy beneath the celebration.

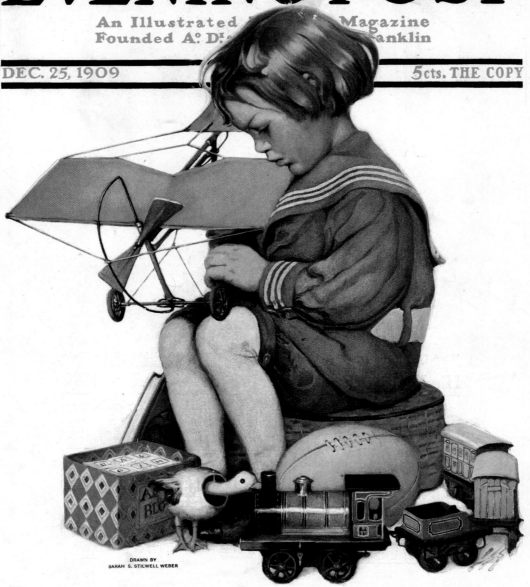

THE SATURDAY EVENING POST

An Illustrated _____ Magazine
Founded A° D _____ ranklin

DEC. 25, 1909   5cts. THE COPY

DRAWN BY
SARAH S. STILWELL WEBER

More Than a Million and a Quarter Circulation Weekly

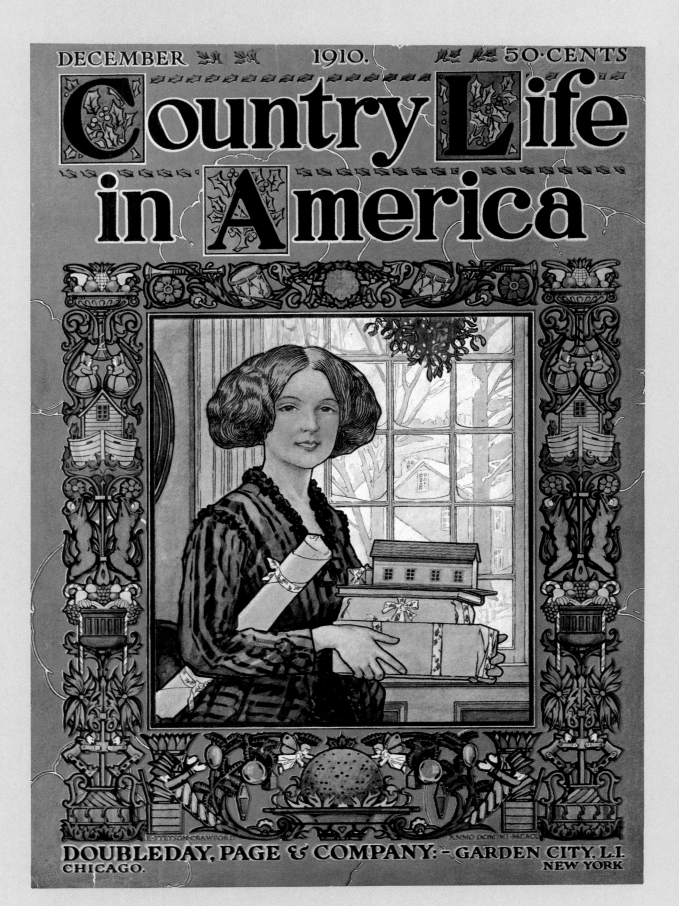

E. Stetson Crawford

Christmas Number

WOMAN'S HOME COMPANION

December, 1915   Fifteen Cents

Beginning
MARGARET DELAND'S *new novel*
"The Rising Tide"

Katherine R. Wireman

Christmas Gifts number of Vogue

December 1 1915

The Vogue Company
CONDÉ NAST   PUBLISHER

Price 25 cents

NEEDLECRAFT

DECEMBER 1928   MAGAZINE   TEN CENTS

ALICE BEACH WINTER

Alice Beach Winter

THE
FARMER'S WIFE
The Magazine for Farm Women

DECEMBER
NINETEEN THIRTY

Merry Christmas!

OVER 950,000
COPIES A MONTH

Haskell Coffin

M^cCALL'S

DECEMBER 1930   TEN CENTS

MEET THE SMITHS
-OF RUSSIA

a sensational revelation of the life
of women under the Soviet
by HELEN CHRISTINE BENNETT

A modern Christmas story
by TEMPLE BAILEY

Neysa McMein

december 1933   10 cents

SUNSET

IN THE BEST HOMES IN THE WEST

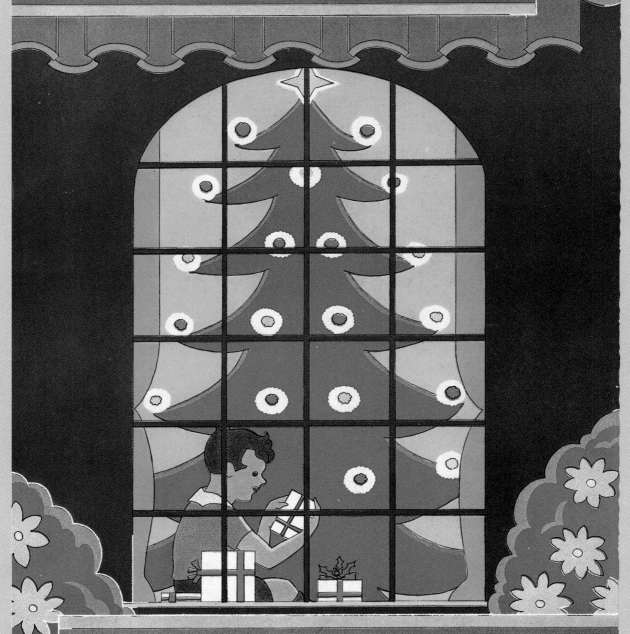

Saying Merry Christmas to SUNSET'S 200,000 Western Families.

Heath Anderson

Woman's Home
Companion

Fifteen Cents in Canada

DECEMBER · 1933 · 10 · CENTS

CHRISTMAS · NUMBER

CHRISTMAS · NUMBER

CHRISTMAS · NUMBER

WOMAN'S WORLD

DECEMBER · 1934   10 CENTS A COPY

GOOD CHRISTMAS STORIES — A CHRISTMAS PLAY
Fashions — Cookery — Homemaking — Needlework — Humor

Miriam Story Hurford   72

LADIES' HOME JOURNAL

DECEMBER 1935 10 CENTS
VOLUME LII, NO. 12 · CANADA 15 CENTS (INCLUDING TAX)

DOROTHY CANFIELD FISHER · DEEMS TAYLOR · PHYLLIS DUGANNE

Eugene Iverd

The Joy of Christmas

Childhood is the time when we are most likely to be engulfed by surges of pure joy, and Christmas is a time when such occurrences are likely. Adults are prone to social conformity, and most frequently find joy as part of a group. Inasmuch as Christmas is a time for parties, dinners, and other gatherings, it is also a time for frequent explosions of joy. An illustrator faces a difficult challenge in portraying joy. Smiles can be shown, and laughter can be portrayed, but it is difficult to avoid the fake or the grotesque. The best artists find ways around this difficulty; their depictions of delight are convincing, and encourage us to join in the happy mood.

Articles By and About { LONGFELLOW, LEW WALLACE, MARY ANDERSON, PAUL LAURENCE DUNBAR / LOUISA ALCOTT, MARY E. WILKINS, F. HOPKINSON SMITH, MRS. S. T. RORER

THE LADIES' HOME JOURNAL

DECEMBER   1898   TEN CENTS

CHRISTMAS NUMBER

THE CURTIS PUBLISHING COMPANY, PHILADELPHIA

James Montgomery Flagg

THE DELINEATOR

DECEMBER, 1917.   15 CENTS A COPY, $1.50 A YEAR   ($2.00 A YEAR IN CANADA)   THE BUTTERICK PUBLISHING COMPANY, NEW YORK

THE CHRISTMAS-TREE FAIRY: PAINTED BY SARAH STILWELL WEBER

 # CHRISTMAS 1917

VOGUE

NOTICE TO READER
When you finish reading this magazine place a 1c. stamp on this notice, mail the magazine and it will be placed in the hands of our soldiers or sailors destined to proceed overseas. No wrapping, no address.—A. S. Burleson, Postmaster-General.

The Vogue Company

Helen Dryden

William Allen White—Heywood Broun—Walter Prichard Eaton

Judge

George Jean Nathan   DECEMBER 24, 1921

James Montgomery Flagg   PRICE 15 CENTS

A CHRISTMAS EAVESDROPPER

Woman's Home Companion

Christmas

December 1928   Ten Cents

     Maginel Wright Barney

The All-America Football Team

December 30, 1933

NRA MEMBER U.S. WE DO OUR PART

Collier's
NATIONAL WEEKLY

5¢ a copy
10c in Canada

Elbert McGran Jackson

J.C. Leyendecker

 # The Birthday of the Christ Child

Today many of us overlook the religious origins of Christmas. We embrace it as a secular celebration, and wish each other "Season's Greetings" rather than a "Merry Christmas." This was less true in the first half of the 20th century. America was then less inclusive, more homogeneous, more churchgoing, and Christianity was, essentially, our national religion.

The most frequent sacred subject for December was the Madonna and Child. Jessie Willcox Smith and J.C. Leyendecker, two of our greatest magazine cover illustrators, made many covers portraying this lovely subject. Despite the acceptability of religious covers in this era, they were not common choices. Most magazines stressed gift giving, tree decoration, and other more mundane and commercial aspects of the season.

E. Reindel

THE MENTOR 25¢

DECEMBER 1929

The Virgin with the pagan halo

G. de Zayas

William P. Welsh

Good Housekeeping

DECEMBER 1931   25 CENTS

DECEMBER 1931
VOL.XCIII NO.6

GOOD HOUSEKEEPING

FIFTY-SEVENTH STREET AT EIGHTH AVENUE, NEW YORK.

EVERY ADVERTISEMENT
GUARANTEED

KATHLEEN NORRIS' Story of Love on a Budget

Margaret W. Jackson + Coningsby Dawson + Achmed Abdullah
Rebecca Hooper Eastman + Emma-Lindsay Squier

Jessie Willcox Smith

J.C. Leyendecker

# Other Themes

Strong customs are fueled by strong conventions. People do not carve faces on watermelons at Halloween. They do not color potatoes at Easter. Modern woman, as liberated as she may be from the past, tends to conform and wear a long white dress when she marries. Christmas offers us a set of rituals with little opportunity for improvisation. The illustrators who made these magazine covers had very little scope in subject matter. The best of them found truth, humor, and emotion in the familiar.

In the search for the covers for this book I was surprised, despite all I have said above, by the persistent recurrence of a few themes. Here in this last section I have gathered some strays– those that didn't fit into any of my nine categories. As might be expected there is more freshness when the illustrator tries a slightly different approach. Santa Clauses and happy children and decorated trees can be manufactured without much inspiration. Covers with less common subjects show the effect of thematic stimulation.

253. Harper's Weekly *Dec. 1898* Edward Penfield *USA*

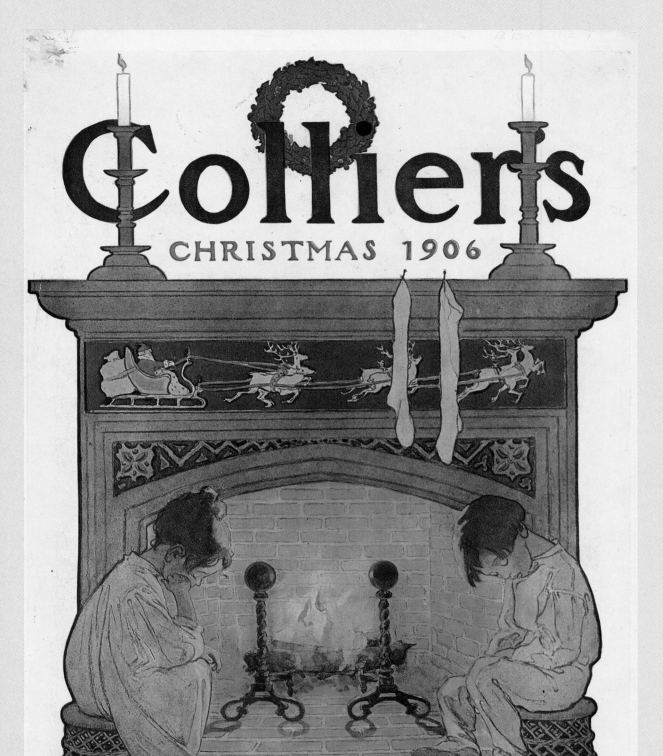

THE SATURDAY EVENING POST

An Illustrated Weekly
...ed A.º D.ⁱ 1728 by Benj. Franklin

5c.

DECEMBER 18, 1915

DRAWN BY
SARAH S. STILWELL WEBER

IN THIS NUMBER: Samuel G. Blythe—Joseph Hergesheimer—Maximilian Foster—Roger W. Babson
William Brown Meloney—Harry Stillwell Edwards—Melville Davisson Post—Pelham Grenville Wodehouse

PRICE 10 CENTS

Vol. 70, No. 1834.   December 20, 1917

Copyright, 1917, Life Publishing Company

Life

THE CHRISTMAS FOREST

Unknown

The Literary Digest

(Title Reg. U.S. Pat. Off.)

THE STORY OF CHRISTMAS—by Norman Rockwell

New York FUNK & WAGNALLS COMPANY *London*

PUBLIC OPINION *New York* combined with *The* LITERARY DIGEST

Vol. 71, No. 13.   Whole No. 1653   December 24, 1921   Price 10 Cents

THE CHRISTMAS NUMBER
PICTORIAL REVIEW

TWENTY-FIVE CENTS   DECEMBER 1921

Charles Twelvetrees

Modern Priscilla

N. S. E.

Needlework — Fashions — Fiction — Housekeeping

December 1922
Twenty Cents

The *Christmas* Ladies' HOME JOURNAL

10 CENTS *By subscription $1.00*
In the United States and in Canada

DECEMBER, 1926
Volume XLIII, Number 12

10¢

PAINTED FOR
THE LADIES' HOME JOURNAL
BY J. KNOWLES HARE

THE LUCK PIECE: By Joseph C. Lincoln

Also Beginning in This Issue: A GREAT SERIES ON THE HOLY LAND, BY HARRY EMERSON FOSDICK; ILLUSTRATED IN COLOR BY HENRY J. SOULEN. *Other Color Features:* GARI MELCHERS, PRUETT CARTER, NORMAN ROCKWELL, H. WILLEBEEK LE MAIR, OLIVER HERFORD and HENRY RALEIGH

THE CURTIS PUBLISHING COMPANY, PHILADELPHIA

PEOPLE'S HOME JOURNAL

Founded 1885

Ten Cents   *December 1928*

1932   DECEMBER   50 cts.

JOHN MARTIN'S
BOOK
THE
CHILD'S
MAGAZINE

LOUISE ROBERTS

A. Petruccelli

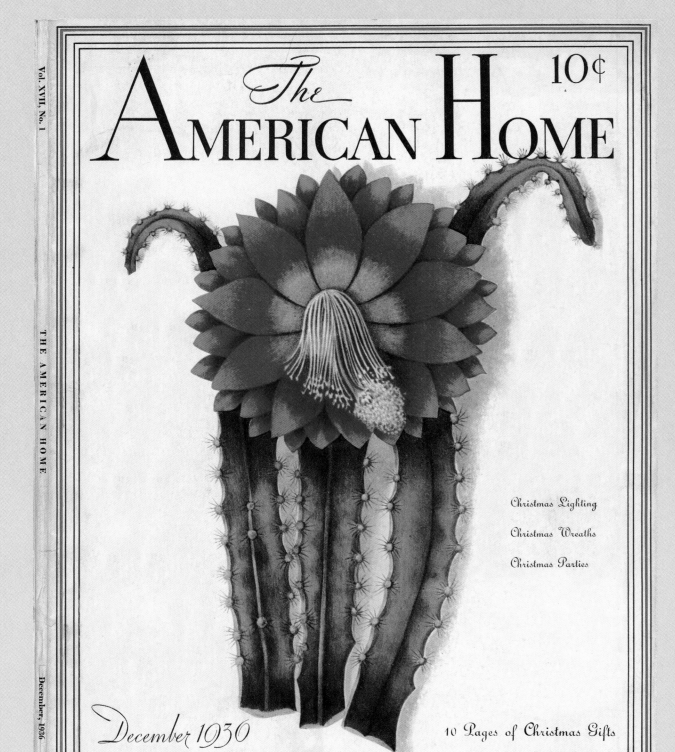

The
AMERICAN HOME

10¢

Christmas Lighting

Christmas Wreaths

Christmas Parties

December 1936

10 Pages of Christmas Gifts

Country Gentleman

AMERICA'S FOREMOST RURAL MAGAZINE

DECEMBER, 19__

In Country Gentlewoman: **MRS. APPLEYARD'S CHRISTMAS DINNER**

Rockwell Kent

Merry